NATURE'S BEST HOMES

HOW ANIMALS' HABITATS HELP THEM LIVE, BREED AND RAISE YOUNG

TOM JACKSON

{CONTENTS}

EVOLUTION

Evolution is the process by which living things can change gradually. Over millions of years, many tiny changes add up to some big differences. Evolution is why there are so many different species living on Earth. Some species are more closely related than others. In 1859, Charles Darwin said that related species had evolved from the same ancestor in the past. He explained how evolution could do that by a process called natural selection.

Making a home takes a lot of hard work, as this busy weaverbird shows.

Animals in a species may look the same, but they all have a unique set of variations. These differences make some animals 'fitter' than others. The fitter ones are better at surviving in wild conditions than others. Darwin said that nature 'selects' these fit animals; they have many children, while the unfit ones die off. Over time, the characteristics that make an animal fit become more common, and eventually every member of the species has them – the species has evolved a tiny bit.

It is not just the way animals look that can evolve. Natural selection also changes the way they behave. The creatures in this book have evolved many unique ways of building homes. Some build complicated dens and nests, while others carry their homes around with them. Each animal uses its home in different ways. As well as providing a place to rest and stay warm, a home is also a hideout from predators, a place from which to launch ambushes or a cosy nursery for young. Let's take a look at some of Nature's Best Homes!

CLOWNFISH

The clownfish sets up home in a sea anemone, a relative of the jellyfish with hundreds of stinging tentacles that fire poisoned darts into any animal that touches it. The clownfish has a thick layer of slime on its skin that protects it from the stings. The clownfish does not stray far, and if danger appears, it dashes back to the safety of the anemone. In return for protection, the clownfish cleans the anemone's tentacles.

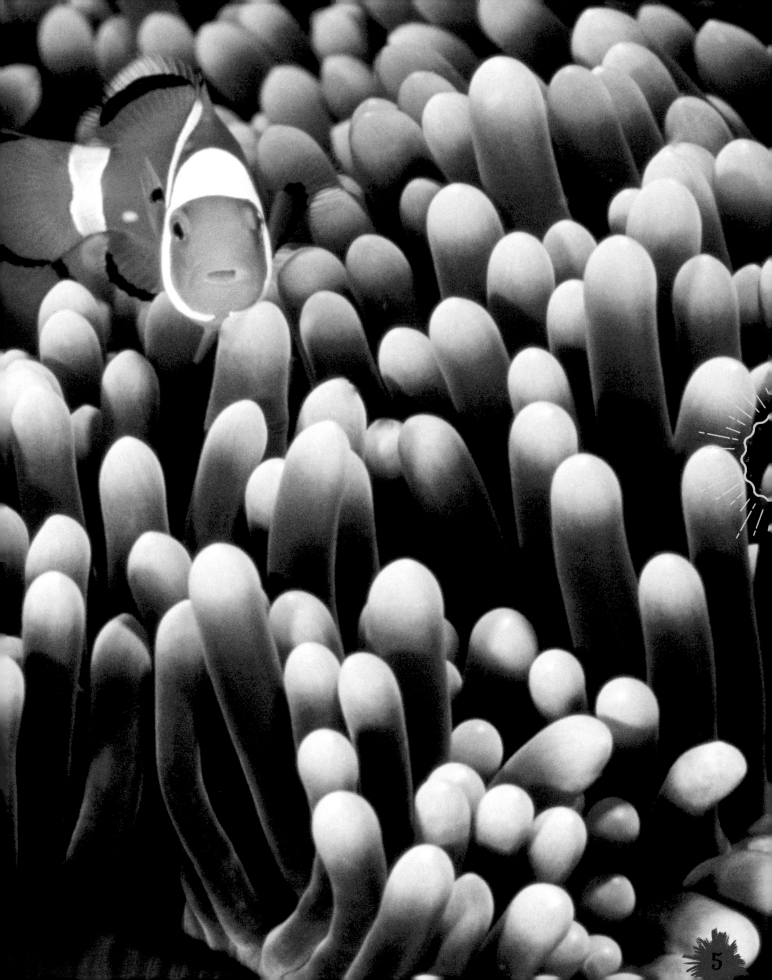

GOLDEN EAGLE

A golden eagle's home is called an 'eyrie'. This is a huge ramshackle nest of twigs built on a cliff ledge. The nest can be bigger than a bath tub and some are more than 100 years old.

Golden eagles are some of the largest birds of prey. They live in mountainous areas and hunt by swooping down from the sky to snatch prey from the ground. They will attack anything from a rabbit to a lamb, taking it back to their eyrie to eat.

An eyrie is a messy tangle of twigs and grass. There are often scraps of fur and bones scattered around, too.

EVOLUTION SOLUTION

Golden eagles hunt animals that live on the ground, swooping down from above to grab prey. That means they are most successful in mountainous areas where they can scan the ground from high perches. As a result, natural selection favoured the birds that built their nests there, too. Any eagles that made nests low down would have spent a lot of time flying up and down, putting them at a disadvantage.

FACTS AND FIGURES

Scientific name........ Aquila chrysaetos

Location................. Northern hemisphere

Habitat.................................... Mountains

Size............................... 2m wingspan

Food.. Rodents, rabbits, birds and lambs

Lifespan...................................30 years

Young............. Eggs laid in remote eyrie

A golden eagle's nest is on a cliff ledge where foxes and other predators cannot reach it. Each generation of eagles use the same ledges and nests as their ancestors, adding new material. As a result, some nests are very old and very large. The biggest are about 1.5m wide and may be 1m deep.

PARROTFISH

These large fish are colourful like a parrot, but they get their name from the beak-like teeth at the front of their mouth. By day, parrotfish scrape food from the rocks in coral reefs. At night they go to sleep inside a bag of snot!

Parrotfish are mostly plant eaters. They scrape away at the tiny algae that grow on the rocks, but they eat whatever else is there as well. Most fish feed during the day; when it gets dark they find shelter under a rock and go to sleep. Not every fish around the reef goes to sleep, though. Sharks patrol, sniffing out sleeping fish. To stay safe, the parrotfish's skin produces a large amount of mucus. This forms a bag around the fish, sealing in the fish's smell. The parrotfish can go to sleep safely without a shark tracking it down.

EVOLUTION SOLUTION

All fish produce mucus on their skin. This is to stop water from inside their bodies leaking out into the salty seawater, and it also makes it harder for worms and other parasites to hang on to the fish's skin. Parrotfish skin makes mucus for all these reasons but the fish has evolved another use for it – to form a smell-proof sleeping bag!

Parrotfish swallow many small chunks of rock as they feed. This does them no harm – the fish just crunch up the rock and poo it out as grains of sand.

FACTS AND FIGURES

Scientific name	Scaridae family
Location	Indian and Pacific oceans
Habitat	Coral reef
Size	30–130cm
Food	Algae
Lifespan	7 years
Young	Eggs float in the water

The slime bag acts like an early warning system. It wobbles if anything touches it, and that wakes up the fish inside.

WASP

For many of us a wasp is just an annoying – and a bit of a scary – stinging insect that buzzes around on summer days. However, these black and yellow minibeasts are among the animal world's best homemakers. They construct elaborate nests out of paper!

Like ants and bees, common wasps live in a colony, ruled over by a queen. A wasp colony needs a big nest and this is usually hung from a tree branch. The queen starts the nest off, building small rooms, or cells, for her young to develop inside. After about a month of hard work, the queen has enough daughters – nearly all wasps are female – to take over the work. The nest hangs from a stalk that is stuck to the branch. The stalk needs to be strengthened as the worker wasps add more cells.

A wasp's nest is made of galleries of six-sided cells.

TEMPORARY STRUCTURE
A big nest may house 1,000 wasps by the end of the summer! However, it is only built to last for one year.

FACTS AND FIGURES

Scientific name............................ Vespula
Location..................................... Worldwide
Habitat.................. Forests, woodlands, parks and gardens
Size.................................. 12-17mm
Food.................................... Insects
Lifespan.......................... less than 1 year
Young................ Queen lays hundreds of eggs in nest

The cells are arranged in clusters, called galleries. Eventually, the whole nest will be covered in an outer wall, with an entrance at the bottom.

The entire structure is made from paper. The wasps make this paper in the same way that humans do. They scrape fibres of wood from the surrounding trees and chew them into a pulp. The wasps then shape the wet pulp into the walls and other elements of their nests. The pulp dries out to become papery and solid. On its own, this material is very brittle, but when connected as cells and galleries it forms a surprisingly strong structure.

Worker wasps are hunters, but don't eat their insect prey. They feed it to the young back in the nest and then drink the babies' liquid poo!

EVOLUTION SOLUTION

Worker wasps have evolved to never have their own young. Instead, they spend their lives helping their mother, the queen, raise hundreds of worker sisters. This system evolved because it guarantees that the queen can produce many new queens. In autumn, dozens of young queens will leave the colony and will each try to start a new colony the following year. The job of this year's colony complete, the workers then gradually die.

A worker wasp will scrape fibres from any wooden structure – such as this fence post.

CADDISFLY

An adult caddisfly looks like a tiny moth. They flutter around streams and ponds, and only live for a short amount of time. Their young, or larvae, live underwater, and build complex homes from silk and any objects they can find.

As well as helping to collect food, the caddisfly's case is a well-camouflaged hiding place.

When it is time to become an adult, the caddisfly larvae closes up the holes in its case to create a sealed cocoon. Then, it transforms in the cocoon.

EVOLUTION SOLUTION

Some of the first insects to evolve probably looked – and lived – a lot like caddisflies. That makes the caddisfly's case an interesting evolutionary mystery. Did the insects first evolve a case for catching food? Or did the case evolve as a safe place to transform into an adult? Today, the case is used for both but no one knows which function developed first.

FACTS AND FIGURES

Scientific name...................... Trichoptera
Location.................................. Worldwide
Habitat......................... Ponds and rivers
Size..................................... 3–15mm
Food................ Larvae are filter feeders
Lifespan........... Adults live for 2 weeks
Young................Lays eggs on plants and rocks under water

Caddisfly larvae are filter feeders. This means they collect tiny scraps of food by 'sifting' them out of the water around them. They build homes to help them do this. Some types of caddisfly weave a funnel-shaped net out of slimy silk produced by glands in their mouth. The silken funnel acts as a net to gather food. Other caddisflies build a house out of pebbles, shells and sticks that litter the riverbed. They glue these items together with silk to form a tube-shaped case with openings at both ends. Inside, the larva wiggles its abdomen to draw a current of water through the house, bringing any food with it.

TRAPDOOR SPIDER

Trapdoor spiders do not build webs to catch prey. They spend their time inside a secret lair, where they wait just below the surface to snatch their prey.

FACTS AND FIGURES

Scientific name.......... Ctenizidae family
Location.................................... Worldwide
Habitat................................... Sandy areas
Size... 25mm
Food... Insects
Lifespan................................. 5-20 years
Young .... Lays eggs in burow

The trapdoor fits the burrow perfectly. It is shaped by a covering of silk and has a silken hinge.

Trapdoor spiders are small, chunky spiders with a powerful bite. They are harmless to humans, but their venom is deadly to insect prey. The spider rarely leaves its home, which is a 25cm-deep burrow. If threatened, the spider scuttles to the bottom of the burrow, but the rest of the time it is stationed by the entrance. This is covered by a trapdoor made of earth. During the day the trapdoor is shut, but at night the spider pokes out its hairy front legs. These can pick up the vibrations of an approaching insect. If one blunders too close, the spider rushes out and hauls it through the trapdoor.

EVOLUTION SOLUTION

All spiders are hunters. They have different ways of catching something to eat. Some spiders chase their prey, some snare them in webs, and some ambush their prey. The trapdoor spider is an ambush hunter. However, the spiders need to protect themselves from hunters as well. The trapdoor and burrow system evolved as a place to hide from predators and prey alike.

COMPASS TERMITE

If you are ever lost in the Australian Outback, termites can help you figure out which way to go. Compass termites build their tall, pointed mounds in line with Earth's magnetic field. They do this to stop their giant mud homes from getting too hot.

Individual worker termites are very weak and puny insects. However, working together in their thousands they can build some of nature's most elaborate nests.

A compass termite mound looks like a huge slab of mud. It is always higher than it is wide, and can be 4m tall and 2.5m across. However, the slab is rarely more than 1m thick, and tapers to a narrow edge. There are many thousands of termites hard at work inside a network of tunnels and chambers. The termites work together to raise the young of their mother and father – the queen and king termites.

Termites need their nest to stay at a regular temperature, and this is where its shape and direction is important. The wide sides always face east and west, with the narrow ends lined up north to south. At night, the mound loses some of its heat. In the morning, the low sun shines on the eastern

All the termite mounds are facing the same way.

The termites make their own haystacks by drying out grass they have collected. Hay is their main food source.

FACTS AND FIGURES

Scientific name	Amitermes
Location	Australia
Habitat	Semi-desert
Size	5mm
Food	Grass and hay
Lifespan	40 days
Young	Queen produces up to 30,000 eggs per day

EVOLUTION SOLUTION

Mound-building termites have evolved many other ways of controlling the temperature inside their homes. Most of the termites live in tunnels beneath ground level, where the deepest chambers are dug into cool, damp soil. Warm air higher up the mound rises through chimneys. This flow pulls chilled air up from lower down.

side and warms up the mound. By the middle of the day, the sun is shining down on to the top of the mound. Only the narrow edge is in direct sunlight during the hottest time of day. As the Sun sets in the west, it warms the western side a little before nightfall. In this way, the mound gets just enough heat for the termites inside but does not get baked in the middle of the day.

MAGNET DETECTOR
In an experiment, termites built their mounds in the wrong direction when a powerful magnet was placed nearby.

GORILLA

The gorillas are some of our nearest relatives, along with chimpanzees and orang-utans. They live in the thick jungles of Central Africa, and know how to make themselves comfortable. Every night, they settle down to sleep in a freshly made bed.

There are two main species of gorilla (some scientists believe there are more) inhabiting different parts of the African forest. However, they all live in the same way. Most of the day is spent eating leaves and fruits collected in the forest. Every day, the leader of the group, or troop, will lead his gorillas to a new feeding site nearby, where there is plenty of fresh food. As the Sun sets, the gorillas get

One of the ways scientists know the number of gorillas in an area is by counting their nests.

EVOLUTION SOLUTION

Gorillas are not the only primates to build nests — all other apes do, too. Primates evolved from small, nocturnal tree-living animals. These ancestors built nests to hide their babies at night while they went out feeding. It was safer to move to a new nest regularly, so predators did not learn where the young were. Likewise, gorillas only sleep in each nest once to avoid predators.

FACTS AND FIGURES

Scientific name	Gorilla species
Location	Central Africa
Habitat	Rainforest
Size	1.8m
Food	Leaves and fruit
Lifespan	40 years
Young	1 baby born every three years

ready to sleep by each building themselves a nest. The nest is made from piles of folded branches and leaves. Most of the time gorillas nest on the ground, but if they find a comfy tree they will build one up there. Gorillas never reuse a nest and always build a fresh one, even for an afternoon nap.

OROPENDOLA

Oropendolas are rainforest birds who build elaborate basket nests that hang from tree branches. Only the females construct these amazing homes, and they hang them all together to form a large colony.

It is normal for one tree to have a couple of dozen nests but some colonies contain 150!

There are about 10 species of oropendola and they all build the same kinds of long, dangling nests. Outside the breeding season, the males and females travel far and wide looking for insects and fruits to eat, but when it is time to mate, the females begin to construct their nests. They are made from long pieces of vine that are carefully woven together. The result is a teardrop-shaped basket that can be 2m long. There is room for one bird and a couple of eggs inside the hollowed-out bulb. The males do not help with nest building. Instead, they spend their time making noisy displays to attract a mate.

Oropendola males are twice the size of the females, so are too heavy for the hanging nests. They roost on branches instead.

FACTS AND FIGURES

Scientific name.................. Psarocolius
Location....... Central and South America
Habitat................................... Rainforest
Size.. 25–35cm
Food................. Insects, seeds and fruit
Lifespan.......................................15 years
Young..................... 2 eggs laid each year

EVOLUTION SOLUTION

Like oropendolas, many birds have evolved to gather as colonies during the breeding season. Forming a big group makes it less likely that the helpless chicks will be eaten. Even if a predator did get into the colony, it would soon eat its fill — and could not eat all the young!

Many male animals show off to females to prove that they are attractive mates. However, few show off as much as the bowerbird. These songbirds from Australia and New Guinea build large tent-like nests out of twigs. They then decorate the nest with whatever brightly coloured objects they can find – petals, mushrooms, berries, even metal cans and pieces of plastic. The bird then displays in front of his palace, hoping to impress a mate.

ACACIA ANT

These tiny ants do not need to build themselves a nest. Acacia trees provide a place for them to live. The tree even supplies the ants with food. In return, the ants defend the tree from other bugs trying to eat its leaves or fruits.

The bullhorn acacia tree is named after the shape of its large thorns. These thorns are hollow inside; acacia ants cut tiny entrance holes to set up home inside them. The ants live in a small colony, with the queen laying her eggs inside the thorns, and workers raising the young. Soldier ants patrol the tree and sting any animal they come across – even goats. The tree's leaves have fleshy tips packed full of oils and proteins. Older worker ants harvest these food parcels to feed the colony.

The acacia's thorns do more than just prick browsing animals; they house an army of defenders!

EVOLUTION SOLUTION

The acacia tree and its army of ants are an example of co-evolution, where two different species have evolved to rely on each other. The acacia ants cannot live anywhere apart from on bullhorn acacias and related trees. When a tree does not house any ants, it struggles as well because other animals eat its leaves.

FACTS AND FIGURES

Scientific name............ Pseudomyrmex
Location........ North and South America
Habitat.......................... Acacia woodlands
Size.. 3mm
Food............ Leaf nodules and honeydew
Lifespan.................................... 40 days
Young............ Queen lays 20 eggs a day

Each thorn has room for about 20 young.

STINKPOT

Turtles and tortoises are famous for carrying their homes around with them in the form of an armoured shell. Many types can pull their legs and head inside the shell for extra protection. The stinkpot, or musk turtle, defends its home in another way.

Stinkpots live in rivers and lakes. Baby stinkpots can hide inside their shells, but as they grow larger, the shell does not keep pace. It still provides a sturdy shield around the body, but there is less room to pull in the appendages. Instead, the turtle has evolved another way of staying safe. When disturbed, it squirts a foul-smelling liquid (or musk) from glands around the edge of its shell. The stench makes the turtle seem a lot less tasty to predators.

FACTS AND FIGURES

Scientific name.. Sternotherus odoratus
Location............................ North America
Habitat......................... Lake and ponds
Size...................................... 5–14cm
Food.................................Shellfish, plants and insects
Lifespan....................................50 years
Young.......1–9 eggs buried in river bank

EVOLUTION SOLUTION

Turtles that spend a lot of time swimming have evolved small, streamlined shells. This sleek shell gives the legs more room to move in water; a heavy, armoured shell would make the animal sink. Although the shell gives some protection, it is not as safe as the large, rounded shells of land tortoises. That is why the stinkpot has evolved its smelly defence system.

Adult stinkpots walk along the bottom of ponds as they hunt for shellfish.

PRAIRIE DOG

Despite the name, these animals are actually a kind of large ground squirrel. They get their name from the yelping bark noises they make – and because they live on the North American prairies. Prairie dogs live burrows, and their tunnel networks are so large and well organised, they are known as 'towns'.

The mounds at the entrance to a burrow make good lookout points, and also stop floodwater from getting into the tunnels.

A prairie dog town may have 400 residents or more. They live in a very organised society, with every prairie dog belonging to a clan, which is a family group with about 20 members. Each clan rules over a patch of grass above ground and lives in burrows below. Only members of the clan are allowed into the grassy area, and into the tunnels underneath. The burrows of neighbouring clans do join up, but the town is not one huge tunnel network. Instead, it is divided into several smaller units called wards.

Prairie dogs build tunnels because they have nowhere else to hide above ground. They dig using the claws on their front paws, flinging the soil out behind them. They then turn around and use their heads to bulldoze the earth out of the burrow, creating a mound around the entrance. Prairie dogs sleep in the deepest chambers at night. During the day they feed on the ground, and if danger threatens, they dash back to the burrow and hide in emergency shelters dug just below the surface.

EVOLUTION SOLUTION

The complicated society of prairie dogs evolved as a balance between two competing goals. Living in a big town is safer than being alone. When a predator approaches, neighbours send out a warning to each other. However, male prairie dogs do not want their females mating with anyone else, and so the clan system evolved where outsiders must stay out of other groups' territories.

PRAIRIE DOG MEGACITY
In the late 19th century, one prairie dog town in Texas, USA, was reported to be 400km long and 160km wide!

FACTS AND FIGURES

Scientific name	Cynomys
Location	North America, Europe, Asia
Habitat	Prairie
Size	30-40cm
Food	Grass
Lifespan	3-5 years
Young	4 pups born each year

Members of the same clan 'kiss' each other hello. In fact, they are giving each other a good sniff to check that they belong to the right group.

WEAVER ANT

Colonies of these ants live in trees. There may be several queens in each colony with thousands of workers. Instead of all living together, the ants construct a tent village with dozens of separate homes. The tents are made from leaves that are glued together in a very unusual way.

Weaver ant homes are chambers made from several glued leaves. It takes hundreds of ants working together to build one. First, the leaves need to be pulled into position. The ants form

New nests are needed as older ones dry out and break.

To get a larva to produce sticky silk, the worker taps it on the head.

a pyramid to reach across the gap from one leaf to another. When the ants have brought the edges of two leaves together, they need to glue them. The weaver ants do this using silk secreted by the larvae, the baby ants. The larvae are wiped along the leaves like living glue sticks!

EVOLUTION SOLUTION

Spiders are famous for using silk, but insects and other bugs use it, too. Silk is a liquid filled with proteins that forms solid strands when it meets the air. It is thought that silk evolved in various ways because insects make it very differently to spiders. For instance, adult insects cannot make silk, only the larvae. This is why weaver ants have to use their young's silk to stick their nests together.

FACTS AND FIGURES

Scientific name..................... Oecophylla
Location.........Africa, Australia and Asia
Habitat.. Forest
Size.. 5–6mm
Food....................................... Insects
Lifespan...................................... 40 days
Young............. Multiple queens lay eggs

ARCTIC FOX

Most foxes dig their own den or move into a burrow that has been abandoned by another animal. However, Arctic foxes live in a land where most of the ground is frozen solid.

Even in the Arctic, there are a few places where the ground thaws out in summer. Arctic foxes dig their dens wherever they find these sheltered spots. However, there are hardly any of them, so once a den has been established, Arctic foxes live in it for generations. A daughter inherits it from her parents and her children will live there when she has died. Some Arctic fox dens are centuries old. Around the den, the fox droppings and scraps of leftover food added to the soil make it very fertile. As a result, fox dens are often surrounded by undergrowth, whereas the rest of the habitat is pretty bare.

EVOLUTION SOLUTION

The Arctic fox evolved from a fox species that lived in warmer habitats. As a result, it hunts in the same way as other foxes and lives in the same kind of family group. However, natural selection has made the Arctic fox different in some ways. The fox has thick fur on its paws to stop it from slipping on ice. It also has small ears. Big ears would get frostbitten in the Arctic.

The Arctic fox only starts to shiver if the temperature drops below −70°C.

The Arctic fox's den is often on raised ground.

FACTS AND FIGURES

Scientific name..............Vulpes lagopus
Location...................................Arctic
Habitat.....................................Tundra
Size..60cm
Food....................Lemmings, hares, eggs
Lifespan..................................3–6 years
Young................5–8 kits born each year

GOLDEN ORB WEAVER SPIDER

The golden orb weaver builds a web as big as your front door. But, this web is almost impossible to see! The spider itself would cover your hand, and it gives a nasty, poisonous bite. Most of time, the spider catches flying insects, but its silken trap can even snare birds!

These big spiders build the largest and most elaborate capture-webs in the world. The spider sits in the middle during the day, waiting for prey to become trapped. At night – or if disturbed – the spider scuttles over to a hideaway among the leaves on one edge of the web.

The web is built in the gaps between trees, the kind of place flying insects buzz around. It is supported by a scaffold of strands that run across the gap. These can be 3m wide, and the spider gets the first line across by feeding a strand of sticky silk into the air and letting the wind carry it across. The main part of the web is only about 1m wide and hangs from the main bridging line. As with the webs of similar spiders, prey is captured in a spiral of sticky

Only the female spiders grow large; the males are a quarter of the size. Each web may be home to several males who eat the female's leftovers.

EVOLUTION SOLUTION

Golden orb weaver spiders build big webs to catch large flying prey, such as wasps, that are too agile or too tough to be trapped in smaller webs. Even if these insects spot the web, they cannot swoop out of danger – the web is too large. However, big webs have unwelcome visitors, too. Ants attempt to steal captured prey. To prevent this, the spider coats the web in a chemical that ants find disgusting, stopping any raids on the spider's catch.

silk, which shimmers in sunlight. However, there is also a spiral of non-sticky silk which the spider uses to clamber across the web. Most spiders produce colourless silk, but these webs are made with gold-coloured strands. No one knows why for sure but it may be that the silk reflects the green of the surrounding forest better – and that makes the web harder to see.

BARRIER THREADS

The spiders also string threads in front of the main web. Leaves blowing in the wind get stuck, which stops them from destroying the main web.

In 2012, a cape wend on display that was woven from golden orb-weaver silk. It contained more than a million threads and took eight years to produce.

This orb weaver is called the 'man's face spider' in Korea. Can you see why?

FACTS AND FIGURES

Scientific name............................ Nephila
Location...................................... Worldwide
Habitat................................Warm forests
Size................. 10-13cm (including legs)
Food.......... Flying insects, birds, lizards
Lifespan...1 year
Young.................... Egg sac glued to leaf

BADGER

Badgers live all over the world and most kinds live alone in a simple underground den. However, the Eurasian badger lives in groups, or clans, and builds a complex tunnel network called a sett.

Large mounds of earth are formed at each entrance as the sett is enlarged.

The largest setts have as many as 90 tunnels and are more than 10m deep.

A badger clan is made up of about 10 adults and their young. All the members build and maintain the sett and defend the territory around it. The sett is dug into banks of dry soil and is a network of tunnels with several entrances. The tunnels lead to deep chambers where the badgers sleep. The residents keep the sett clean and tidy. The sleeping areas are lined with dried grass, which the badgers carry under their chins. When it gets dirty, the bedding is thrown out. Every sett has a rubbish tip, where the badgers also go to the toilet.

EVOLUTION SOLUTION

Eurasian badgers live in cool damp habitats, such as forests and woodlands. There is plenty of food for them here, so they can live in groups without having to compete with each other over food. Badger species that live in drier areas have to spread out to find enough food, and so it is better that they live alone.

FACTS AND FIGURES

Scientific name.................. Meles meles
Location...........................Europe and Asia
Habitat............................... Woodland
Size......................................68–80cm
Food............... Insects, worms, rodents
Lifespan.......................................14 years
Young.................. 2 or 3 born each year

(HAZEL) DORMOUSE

Although the name may suggest it, the dormouse is not a mouse. In fact, it is more closely related to squirrels. The 'dor' part of the name comes from an old French word for sleepy, and this animal spends a lot of time snoozing in a cosy den.

FACTS AND FIGURES

Scientific name. Muscardinus avellanarius
Location.. Europe
Habitat.................... Bushes and hedges
Size.. 16–9cm
Food.............. Flowers, nuts and berries
Lifespan...................................... 4 years
Young.... 2 litters of 5 young each year

When the dormouse wakes up in spring, it gets its strength back by eating flowers.

A dormouse is a very agile climber and need not come to the ground at all until winter.

The dormouse spends the summer feeding on berries and nuts. It builds itself a nest from strips of bark that it weaves into a hollow ball. The nest is set in a bramble patch, where the thorns will prickle anything that gets close. During cold weather, the dormouse does not get up in the morning and sleeps all day – perhaps longer. As winter approaches, it prepares to hibernate by building a new nest on the ground under leaves. The dormouse sleeps inside for seven months!

EVOLUTION SOLUTION

The dormouse evolved into a hibernator as the best way to survive the winter. In winter, it is dangerously cold to be outside and there is hardly any food to be found. During hibernation, body functions, such as breathing and heart rate, slow down to save energy, so the dormouse can go without feeding for several months.

BEAVER

This big rodent is one of the animal kingdom's top construction experts. It cuts down trees, digs canals and dams rivers. It even makes its own private island – and lives inside!

Beavers live in and around forest rivers. In summer, they eat the lush grasses that grow along the bank, and they make sure they have plenty to eat by building dams to change the flow of the river. In winter, the beavers make do with a supply of rotting wood, which is stored on the riverbed.

The beaver's top teeth rub against the bottom ones, always keeping them razor sharp.

EVOLUTION SOLUTION

The way beavers make their homes has evolved to solve several problems. Damming the river creates a deep pool, and that provides plenty of room for the beaver to build a safe underwater entrance to its lodge. Only the surface of deep water will freeze in winter, and so the entrance is open all year around. This means the beaver can collect its supply of wood food from the pool even when it is iced over.

Two million years ago, giant 2-m-long beavers lived in North America.

All this is possible because beavers are powerful swimmers, and their front teeth are so sharp, they can gnaw through tree trunks!

The beaver's construction job starts in the forest, where they fell small trees and cut them into logs. Some logs are stored for winter, while the beavers pile the rest across the river to build a dam. The dam slows the flow of the water and creates a wide, shallow pool upstream. This creates more bank areas for the grass to grow. The dam also contains stones and mud, and the beaver now makes a large pile of these in the middle of the dam. Next, it dives under the water and burrows into the pile, digging out two rooms inside. The first is where the beaver dries off after swimming in through the underwater entrance. The second is a cosy, dry sleeping area. This is the beaver's lodge. Normally a male and female share the lodge with their young, or kits.

FACTS AND FIGURES

Scientific name	Castor
Location	North America, Europe, Asia
Habitat	Forest rivers and streams
Size	60–90cm
Food	Grass, wood
Lifespan	25 years
Young	2 or 3 kits born in winter

GLOSSARY

Arctic The region around the North Pole. The Arctic is always very cold and frequently frozen over.

canal A water channel dug into the ground.

clan An animal group where related animals and their offspring live together.

colony A large collection of animals that live in the same place and may work together to help in survival.

dam A structure that blocks the flow of a river. The result is a deep pool upstream of the dam.

evolution The process by which animals, plants and other life forms change gradually to adapt to changes in their environment.

habitat The kind of environment that an animal lives in. Each species has evolved to survive in its particular habitat.

hibernation A sleep-like state that some animals enter in winter. Body processes slow down so the animal does not use much energy to stay alive during long, cold periods.

larva A young form of an insect or other invertebrate. The larva looks different to the adult form and lives in a different way.

magnetic field A region of invisible force that surrounds a magnet. The magnetism of Earth surrounds the planet in a magnetic field.

mucus A slimy liquid used by animals to keep body parts moist or create a protective layer.

musk A strong-smelling liquid produced by animals. Musk is used to scare away predators or attract mates.

natural selection The process by which evolution works. Natural selection allows individuals that are good at surviving to increase in number, while those that are less able to compete go down in number.

nocturnal To be active at night.

parasite A life form that survives by stealing resources from another species — their host. Some parasites grow on the outside of their host, others grow inside the body.

predator An animal that hunts and kills other animals for food.

prey An animal that is hunted and killed by a predator.

primate A type of mammal that includes lemurs, monkeys, apes — and humans.

pulp A mixture of wood fibres and water to make a soft gooey material.

scaffold A framework that supports a structure.

solution Something that solves a problem.

species A group of animals that share many characteristics. The main common feature is that members of a species can breed with each other. Members of different species cannot produce young successfully.

tentacle A flexible, armlike feature seen on many different animals, mostly sea creatures.

territory An area that is controlled by an animal or group of animals. The territory is where they find food and build their homes.

FURTHER INFORMATION

BOOKS

THE WORLD IN INFOGRAPHICS: Animal Kingdom,
by Jon Richards and Ed Simkins (Wayland, 2014)

MIND WEBS: Living Things,
by Anna Claybourne (Wayland, 2014)

WHAT IS EVOLUTION?,
by Louise Spilsbury (Wayland, 2015)

WEBSITES

www.zsl.org/kids

The kids' section of the Zoological Society of London's website is packed
with animal information, games and activities, as well as the latest
scientific studies.

www.ngkids.co.uk

Animal-related facts, pictures and games from
the kids' section of the National Geographic website.

www.nhm.ac.uk/kids-only

The Natural History Museum website is filled
with games, facts and information on the world of animals.

INDEX

First published in 2015 by Wayland
Copyright © Wayland, 2015

All rights reserved.

Editor: Julia Adams
Designer: Rocket Design

Dewey number: 591.5'64-dc23
ISBN 978 0 7502 8800 2

Printed in China

10 9 8 7 6 5 4 3 2 1

Picture acknowledgements: Cover: © Gerard Lacz/FLPA; p.1: © Shutterstock; p. 3 © Tony Heald/naturepl.com; pp. 4–5: © David Hall/naturepl.com; p. 6: © Laurie Campbell/naturepl.com; p. 7: © Nature Production/naturepl.com; p. 8, p. 30: © Kim Taylor/naturepl.com; p. 9: © Nick Upton/2020VISION/naturepl.com; p. 10: © Jan Hamrsky/naturepl.com; p. 11: © Hans Christoph Kappel/naturepl.com; p. 12 (top and bottom): © Ingo Arndt/naturepl.com; p. 13: © Owen Newman/naturepl.com; p. 14: © Bernd Rohrschneider/FLPA; p. 15: © Patricio Robles Gil/naturepl.com; pp. 16–17: © Barrie Britton/naturepl.com; p. 18 (top and bottom): © Visuals Unlimited/naturepl.com; p. 19: © Barry Mansell/naturepl.com; p. 20, 21: © Shutterstock; p. 22: © Ann and Steve Toon/naturepl.com; p. 23:
© Paul Nicklen/National Geographic Creative/Corbis; p. 24: © Steven David Miller/naturepl.com; p. 25 (top): © John Calcalosi/naturepl.com; p. 25 (bottom): © Rick Buettner/Alamy; p. 26: © Kevin J Keatley/naturepl.com; p. 27: © Kerstin Hinze/naturepl.com; p. 28: © Vincent Munier/naturepl.com; p. 29: © Orsolya Haarberg/naturepl.com; all images used as graphic elements: Shutterstock.

Wayland, an imprint of Hachette Children's Group
Part of Hodder & Stoughton
Carmelite House
50 Victoria Embankment
London
EC4Y 0DZ

An Hachette UK Company
www.hachette.co.uk
www.hachettechildrens.co.uk